KITCHEN TABLE FUN

Other Books by Joseph Leeming

FUN WITH GREETING CARDS

FUN WITH ARTIFICIAL FLOWERS

FUN WITH SHELLS

FUN WITH WIRE

FUN WITH PENCIL AND PAPER

FUN WITH BEADS

FUN FOR YOUNG COLLECTORS

HOLIDAY CRAFT AND FUN

FUN WITH FABRICS

FUN WITH CLAY

FUN WITH MAGIC

MORE FUN WITH MAGIC

FUN WITH WOOD

FUN WITH LEATHER

FUN WITH STRING

FUN WITH PAPER

FUN WITH PLASTICS

FUN WITH BOXES

THE COSTUME BOOK FOR PARTIES AND PLAYS

FUN WITH PUZZLES

MORE FUN WITH PUZZLES

PAPERCRAFT

Kitchen Table Fun

By AVERY NAGLE

& JOSEPH LEEMING

Illustrated by Jessie Robinson

J. B. Lippincott Company

PHILADELPHIA   NEW YORK

Contents

Acknowledgment

We would like to thank John M. Clapper and his wife, Edna, for their very kind permission to use material that appeared in their extremely helpful and interesting magazine, *Pack-O-Fun, The Only Scrap Craft Magazine.* This magazine, founded and continually improved by the efforts of Mr. and Mrs. Clapper and their helpers, has been of assistance not only to us, but also to thousands of leaders of Boy and Girl Scout groups and other children's and youth organizations. It would be difficult to assess the immense amount of good it has done in the field of crafts and hobbies.

AVERY NAGLE
JOSEPH LEEMING

Foreword

Kitchen Table Fun describes the contents and purpose of this book so clearly that hardly any further explanation is needed. Children love to be in the kitchen while Mother is there—which, alas, often seems to be too many hours a day—and children love to be taught how to make and do new and interesting things. This book is intended, therefore, to be of help in both of these fields of activity.

For the child, it offers many things that are easy to make. For the busy mother, it offers, it is hoped, some surcease from the oft-heard plea of "What can I do now?" or "Let me do something to help."

Everything described is made from articles that are usually found in any kitchen, or can easily be obtained during the day's marketing. These, and one end of the kitchen table, are all that are needed for—with luck—many hours of fun for children, and some greater degree of peace and quiet perhaps, for busy mothers.

AVERY NAGLE
JOSEPH LEEMING

Paper Plates

PASTED PAPER PLAQUES

PASTED PICTURE PLAQUES. Begin by pasting a colored construction paper (or other paper) circle or square to the center of a plate. Then paste on colored pictures cut from magazines or used greeting cards. Pictures from greeting cards are especially good, since they have great variety—flowers, children, kittens, Easter bunnies, landscapes, reproductions of famous paintings, and many, many more are all there for you to use.

Paint the rims of the plates with poster paints or enamel. Cover the front of the plate with clear cellophane. Pull the cellophane tight and fasten its edges to the back of the plate with gummed tape. Add a gummed hanger.

RUFFLE-EDGED PLATES. Use 2 paper plates, each 6 inches in diameter. On one of them paste a colored cut-out picture or a good-looking decal. Sew or cement a ribbon ruffle around the other plate.

The ruffle is the most important part of these plates, and it should be made as carefully as possible. Use 1½ yards of 2-inch ribbon for each plate, and pleat it in box pleats 1 inch apart. This will average 17 pleats for a 6-inch plate. Stitch down the edge of the ruffle, using long basting stitches. If you sew it to the plate, use a heavy needle, since the pressure needed to push it through the two thicknesses

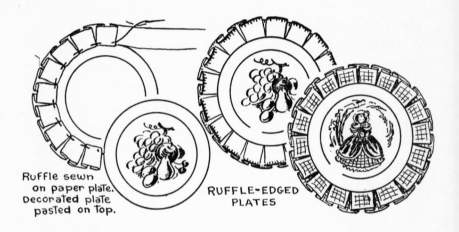

Ruffle sewn on paper plate. Decorated plate pasted on top.

RUFFLE-EDGED PLATES

of ribbon and the plate would break a thin needle. When the ruffle has been put in place, cement the plate with the decal to the front of the ruffle-edged plate. Then put a gummed cloth picture hanger on the back.

The ribbon used for the edging should be bright and gay. Good kinds of ribbon to use include red and white checked taffeta, red and white polka dots, striped ribbon of all kinds, and plain pastels.

You can also use ten-cent-store white china plates for the plate with the decal or picture on it.

PAINTED PLAQUES. Start by collecting suitable designs from magazines, calendars, books, children's coloring books, Christmas cards and other likely sources. Flowers and birds are among the best to use. Paste the designs to white paper. When starting on a plate, put carbon paper on the

PAINTED PLAQUES

plate, carbon side down, and place one of your designs over it—positioned so it will be in the right place in the plate's center. Trace the design onto the plate with a hard pencil. Then color the design. When it is finished, apply a coat of shellac. Leave the plate as it is, or cover its front with clear cellophane.

NAPKIN HOLDER. This is a handy holder in which to keep napkins, notes or grocery bills. Use a colored plate and punch holes halfway around its edge. Button hole with

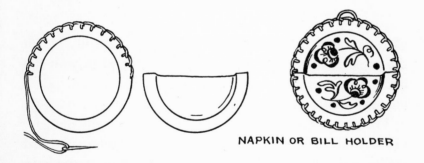

NAPKIN OR BILL HOLDER

yarn of a contrasting color. Do not break the yarn. Cut another colored plate across the middle and place one half on top of the first plate, top sides facing. Punch holes around edge of both plates and buttonhole until you reach the place at which you started. Paste an attractive picture on each plate. Make a hanger by tying ends of piece of yarn around two buttonhole yarns at top, or attach a gummed hanger.

EMBOSSED PLAQUES. You can make raised or embossed designs on paper plates by an easy process. To get the design, you will need a wall plaque or some other object of plaster, metal or pottery that has a raised design on it. There are many such objects, and you should be able to find some in your own home or the home of a friend. If not, look in a ten-cent store.

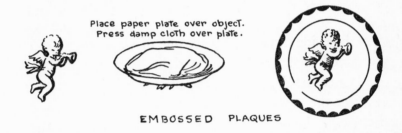

Place paper plate over object.
Press damp cloth over plate.

EMBOSSED PLAQUES

Put the bottom of a paper plate on a raised design. Wet a cloth and wring it as dry as you can with your hands. Then spread the cloth over the inside of the plate and hold it there with one hand. The cardboard will soon become moist. As it does so, press your fingers against it to push it against the high and low parts of the design beneath it.

When you have molded the cardboard to the design, fill the plate with salt. Put a weight on the salt to keep the plate pressed firmly against the design. When the plate has dried out, the design will be permanently embossed on the bottom of the plate.

Paint the design with water colors or poster paints. Paint a colored border around the rim of the plate.

WALL MASKS. You can make any number of different paper plate wall masks. They can show Chinese faces, Spanish dancing girls, your favorite movie stars, or any other kind of face or person you wish. You can obtain many suggestions of faces to copy by looking through magazines and books. If you like *Alice in Wonderland*, for example, you can make wall masks of many of the characters in it.

To make a wall mask, turn a paper plate upside down.

Draw the features on a separate piece of paper or cut them from a colored picture in a magazine, and paste them on the plate. This is done because you cannot draw very well on the rough surface of a paper plate.

You can make the hair from cloth, crepe paper or woolen yarn. You can braid yarn to make pigtails and can curl crepe paper to make brown or yellow curls. The hair has much to do with making the masks look life-like, attractive and interesting. Paper or ribbon flowers and ribbons can be pasted on to make different decorative effects. Cloth kerchiefs can be added, or even cardboard hat silhouettes, decorated with flowers and ribbons.

WALL MASKS

PAPER PLATE GARDEN PLAQUES. If available, use the water-resistant picnic plates for these gardens. These can be covered on both sides with papier-mâché to add strength and make an interesting texture, but it is not absolutely necessary.

Start by covering the upper two-thirds of the plate's center with blue construction paper for the sky. Cover the lower third with green construction paper for grass. This can also be done with poster paints or crayons. Next make the garden, which can be done in many different ways. Here are a few suggestions:

Make a tree for one side of the garden by using twigs from a real tree or wires wrapped with brown or dark green crepe paper for the trunk and branches. The foliage is made from bits of sponge dyed green by dipping them into vegetable coloring or tempera paints mixed with water. Kelly green and Chinese red are among the best colors for trees. Cement the tree to the plate. Perch a small ten-cent-store plastic bird in the tree.

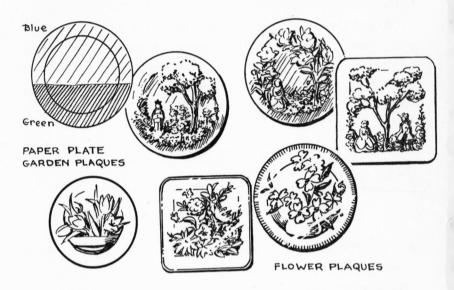

PAPER PLATE GARDEN PLAQUES

FLOWER PLAQUES

Next make the garden, using small artificial flowers. Add a butterfly cut from yellow crepe or tissue paper and cemented to a thin green wire. Put pebbles at the bottom of the garden. The painted grass can be covered with crumpled green tissue paper or green papier-mâché, but this is not absolutely necessary. When the garden is completed, add a small ten-cent-store figurine.

FLOWER PLAQUES. Use a 10-inch plate and paste a circle of colored paper to its center. Using a flower picture from a magazine or greeting card as a model, fasten small dried and pressed flowers or artificial flowers to the plate with small pieces of transparent gummed tape. The flower design may be an attractive bouquet or flowers arranged in a vase or bowl. Cut the vase or bowl from light cardboard. You can also arrange the flowers so they appear to be growing. For some of these plaques, paste two pieces of paper to the plate—one blue for the sky, and the other one green for grass.

With these designs you can use tiny butterflies cut from bright yellow crepe or tissue paper. Cement them to thin green-covered wire and put them amongst the flowers.

When the design is completed, paint the rim of the plate in a harmonizing color. Use enamel or poster paint. Then "glass in" the picture with clear cellophane pulled tight and fastened to the back of the plate with gummed tape. Fasten a gummed hanger to the back.

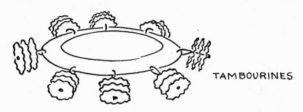

TAMBOURINES

TAMBOURINES. To make a tambourine you will need 24 pop bottle caps. When you have collected these, remove their cork liners, flatten the caps with a hammer, and with a nail punch a hole through the center of each cap. With scissor points, punch 8 holes around the edge of a paper plate. String the caps, 3 to a string, to the holes.

You can make a deeper-toned tambourine by gluing 2 paper plates together face to face and stringing the caps to holes in their edges. To play a tambourine, you shake it to make the caps rattle, hold it in one hand and strike it against the other, also strike it on your elbow and knees.

PAPER PLATE CLOCKS. A fine clock with movable hands can be made very easily from a square or round paper plate and some light-weight cardboard for the hands. Print the numerals for the hours with ink, pencil or crayons. Then cut out the two hands, and fasten them to the center of the plate with a brass paper fastener. Then color the rim of the plate with paints or crayons.

PAPER PLATE CLOCKS

BUTTON CATCH GAME. Draw 3 crayon circles of different sizes on a paper plate to make a target. Print a 1 on the outer circle, a 3 on the middle circle, and a 5 on the inner bull's eye circle. Hold the plate in your hand and put a button on the bull's eye. Jerk your hand upward, so the button flies up in the air. See if you can catch it on the bull's eye. See how many tosses it takes for you to score 10 points.

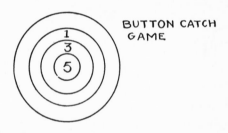

BUTTON CATCH GAME

PAPER PLATE TOSS. Put a waste basket on the floor near one end of the room. From a line 10 feet away, toss paper plates at the basket. Players throw three plates at each turn, and each plate that lands in the basket scores one point. The good part about this game is the difficulty of aiming the paper plates accurately. They will go every which way until you get the knack of controlling them.

Clothespins

CLOTHESPIN
ANIMALS AND BIRDS

CLOTHESPIN ANIMALS AND BIRDS. Any number of different animals and birds can be made from cardboard and spring clip clothespins. You can either draw or trace the animals' heads and bodies, or can cut pictures out of magazines and glue them to cardboard for stiffness.

CLOTHESPIN FISHES. Wooden clothespins are first-class, ready-made fishes with which to play a fishing game. The fishing pole is a stick with a piece of string tied to one end, and a metal nut or bolt tied to the end of the string.

The clothespins are set afloat on water, in a wash tub or whatever other good-sized container you have. The stunt then is to maneuver the string into the slot of the clothespin. When you succeed in doing this, you have hooked your fish and can pull him out of the water. The object of the game is to see who can hook the greatest number of fish.

19

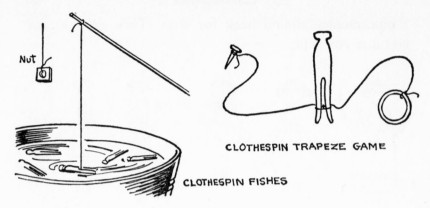

CLOTHESPIN TRAPEZE GAME

CLOTHESPIN FISHES

TRAPEZE GAME. With a clothespin for a handle, a nail and a ring such as a rubber or metal washer or a cut-out circle of cardboard, you can make a trapeze artist game.

Cut a notch near the lower end of the clothespin. Then fasten the nail and washer to it with two pieces of thread, as shown. The nail is now the Man on the Flying Trapeze. The game is to make him swing through the center of the ring. Hold the clothespin between your thumb and fingers and slowly start the nail and ring swinging by slightly moving the clothespin. You will soon find that it is quite a job to get the trapeze artist to pass through the ring.

CRUMB BRUSH

CRUMB BRUSH. This is a useful little brush with which you can sweep up dining table crumbs or use for other purposes. Cut straws from an old broom, arrange them around a clothespin, and tie tightly with wire or strong string. Wind a pipe cleaner around neck for arms. Then dress in any costume you wish.

LAPEL
PINS

LAPEL PINS. Clothespin lapel pins are made of toy clothespins, though regular clothespins sawed in two above the springs may also be used. (See Clothespin People pages 23 and 25.) Dress and decorate the small pins as angels and as people of all kinds. Fasten safety pins to back by passing them through the fabric of a cloth costume or by winding yarn around the safety pins and the clothespins.

BUTTERFLIES

BUTTERFLIES. These big colorful butterflies can be used as wall decorations. Use colored pictures of butterflies from books or magazines as models. Paint a clothespin to be the head and body. Cut wings from a folded piece of crepe paper, tissue paper or ordinary paper. Decorate with paint and stiffen by giving them a coat of shellac on both sides. Slide wings between the prongs of the clothespin. Add feelers of wire or of pipe cleaners. To hang a butterfly on the wall, fasten a gummed paper hanger to the underside of the body. If you want to suspend it from the ceiling or a lighting fixture, push a thumbtack into the clothespin and tie a thread around the tack. Experiment to get the thumbtack in the right place, so the butterfly will be on an even keel.

You can also make smaller butterflies by using toy clothespins.

PICTURE
HOLDER

PICTURE HOLDER. Paint two clothespins with poster paint—any color you wish. Then glue them upside down on a rectangle of heavy cardboard or wood. Paste a picture to cardboard and mount it in the picture holder as shown. You can also make these picture holders of toy clothespins.

RING TOSS. For this game push 4 clothespins into the bottom of a cardboard box, near the corners. Put a fifth clothespin in the center. Then, from a distance of about 10 feet, toss fruit-jar rubbers at the clothespins. Each player throws 5 rubbers at each turn. Each ringer scores 1 point. Ringing all 5 clothespins scores three additional points. If you have no fruit-jar rubbers, make five wire or cardboard rings.

CLOTHESPIN AND BOTTLE GAME. Put an empty quart milk bottle behind a straight-backed chair. Then stand in front of the chair, reach over its back, and try to drop clothespins into the bottle without resting your hands on the chair. Each player drops 10 clothespins at each turn. Each pin that lands in the bottle scores 1 point.

FULL-LENGTH CLOTHESPIN PEOPLE. Clothespin people or dolls can be dressed in dozens of different ways—

in foreign costumes, and as Indians, cowboys, clowns, a Dutch girl and boy, a bride and groom and so on. You can copy some of the many costumes that are pictured in books and magazines.

The easiest dolls to make are those shown at the left of the drawing. For a woman, you paint with poster paints the face and the blouse or part of the costume that is above the waist. A skirt and hat are then made from bits of cloth. For a man, the entire costume is painted, and you need only make a hat of paper or felt. If you do not wish the figures to have hats, hair can be made of yarn, or thread, or by covering the top of the head with glue and dipping it in cornmeal or coffee grounds. Instead of painting the nose, you can glue on a tiny ball of cotton. Pipe cleaner arms can be added and painted to match the rest of the costume. To make these little people stand up, stick their feet into clay or into slits in a small cardboard box cover. You can also cut off the rounded ends of the "feet" and glue or tape the feet to a cardboard or wood square. Cardboard props glued to their backs can also be used. For women's figures make a stiff paper cone and fasten it to the clothespin with adhesive tape. The bottom of the cone should be on a line with the bottoms of the "feet."

More elaborate figures are made by fully clothing both men and women. For these, you can make a head of plastic

FULL-LENGTH CLOTHESPIN PEOPLE

wood or papier-mâché, if you wish. It makes a larger, better shaped head than that of the flat-topped clothespin. In using plastic wood, keep your fingers moist. After the head has dried, sandpaper it with fine sandpaper, since it should be very smooth for the features to be painted on. A good way to make the face is to give it a light wash of pale pink water color and then use water-color pencils to do the features. A tiny ball of cotton can be glued on for the nose. Use pipe cleaners for arms, fastening them just below the neck with gummed tape. Dip the ends in the pink water color to match the face.

The drawings give some suggestions of the almost unlimited possibilities of clothing for the dolls. Women can be dressed in a separate blouse and skirt, or in a one-piece dress made of an oblong of cloth or crepe paper with a hole in the middle to slip over the head. The dress is then gathered at the waist, with a belt or sash made of ribbon, cloth, rickrack or some other material. Trousers for the men dolls are made by cutting out and sewing together a front and back piece of cloth.

Hats are made of felt, paper, light-weight cardboard or straw lace, a material used by many florists. Felt may be blocked for some hats. Cut a circle of felt a little larger than the hat is to be, wet it thoroughly, and pull it down over a clothespin head. Wrap a rubber band around it where the brim will begin. Let the felt dry. Then trim it with scissors, if needed, and make it the shape you wish. Moisten it again if this is needed. Trim women's hats with very narrow ribbons, tiny feathers and flowers, green leaves of felt and other similar materials. Clothespin people can be made of toy clothespins as well as pins of the regular size.

HALF-LENGTH CLOTHESPIN PEOPLE. These clothespin dolls or people are made in the same way as the "full-length" people. But instead of using a whole clothespin, you use only the part above the prongs. The prongs are

HALF-LENGTH CLOTHESPIN PEOPLE

sawed off, leaving a very well-shaped doll's head and body. These are then given pipe cleaner arms and are dressed in any one of a hundred different ways. To use one as a lapel pin, sew a safety pin to the back of the costume. Smaller half-length people are made from toy clothespins.

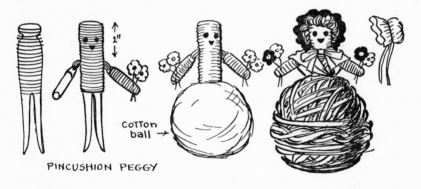

cotton
ball →

PINCUSHION PEGGY

PINCUSHION PEGGY. Peggy is a doll whose skirt is a yarn and cotton pincushion. Her body is a clothespin. Glue one end of brightly colored 2-ply yarn around the clothespin's head and wrap the yarn around the pin down to the beginning of the prongs. Tie 2 medium-sized safety pin arms to the neck with yarn. Wrap each arm with yarn of the same color as the body. Cement small artificial flowers to each hand.

Glue on eyes and mouth of felt or paper. Curl yarn around your finger to make the hair, and glue it to the head. Make a hat of felt. For the skirt, roll cotton into a 2½ inch ball. Coat prongs of pin with glue, and glue on the cotton. Then wind yarn, of a different color than the body, around and around the cotton to make a 3-inch ball skirt. Trim the skirt with stripes of different colored yarns, and finish by gluing a 2-inch cardboard circle to bottom.

CLOTHESPIN BOATS

CLOTHESPIN BOATS. These boats are made from clip clothespins. You can make a whole fleet of them very quickly and easily. To make a boat, remove the clip from a clothespin. Fasten the two flat sides together with airplane cement or waterproof household cement. Cut a piece of paper 2 by 2½ inches for the sail, and slip the sail over a toothpick, as shown. Put the toothpick in the hole in the clothespin hull and the boat is ready to sail.

Glasses
and
Paper Cups

DANCING SEEDS. Seeds will dance in a very lively fashion in a glass of ginger ale or some other carbonated beverage. Drop several apple, lemon or grape seeds into a glass. They will sink and remain at the bottom until carbon dioxide bubbles become attached to them and carry them up to the top. There, some of the bubbles will break away, and the seeds will sink again, only to repeat the performance as long as the bubbles last.

DRINKING GLASS SEA SHELLS. Everybody knows that when you hold large sea shells to your ear, you hear a noise like that of the ocean. You can get just the same effect with an ordinary drinking glass. Hold one close to your ear, and you will see. The reason for this is that the air around you is nearly always full of a mixture of different sounds. When you put a shell or a glass to your ear, what you hear is an amplification of any sound that corresponds to the natural pitch of the shell or glass. You can try this experiment also with tin cans and glass jars.

CLEAR WATER YOU CAN'T SEE THROUGH. Tell your friends that you can fill a glass with clear water, which everybody knows is transparent, but that you can

27

CLEAR WATER YOU
CAN'T SEE THROUGH

arrange things so that they will not be able to see through
the water. You won't put any ink or dye in it, either. The
water will be clear, just as you say. To do the stunt, fill a
glass nearly full of water and put a coin behind it, as shown
in the drawing. Then look at the coin through the top of
the glass, looking through the surface of the water and the
opposite side of the glass. You won't be able to see the coin.

THE MYSTIC GLASS. Whatever is put into this mystic
glass mysteriously disappears immediately afterward. The
secret lies in the use of a hair net, which you can get at a
ten-cent store. Arrange the hair net on the glass, so that its
edges hang over the rim of the glass. Put the glass on a table
and tell your friends that you are going to show them something mysterious. Drop a couple of pennies or buttons into
the glass and cover the glass with a handkerchief. Lift the
handkerchief, lifting the net with it. The net will bring along
the pennies or buttons, hidden within the folds of the handkerchief.

TURNING THE TUMBLERS. This stunt is done with
three glasses or tumblers. Put them on a table, as shown in
drawing 1. The center one is mouth up, and the two end
ones are mouth down. Tell your friends to watch you carefully. You then take a glass in each hand and quickly turn
them over. You repeat this movement twice and all the glasses
are mouth up. Then turn the center glass mouth down and

challenge a friend to try it. Try as he will, he will never be able to bring the three glasses mouth up by turning two at a time. The reason for this is that the stunt must be started with the center glass mouth up and the end glasses mouth down. The drawings show how the moves are made that make the stunt work. Practice it a few times and you will have a stunt that can give you fun for a long time.

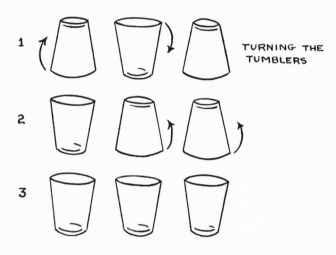

TURNING THE TUMBLERS

DRINKING GLASS CATCH. Say to a friend, "Did you know that I can stay under water for a whole minute?" When he says he doesn't believe it, take him to the kitchen, fill a glass of water at the sink and hold it over your head.

MAGIC PAPER CUP. This is a magic paper cup into which you drop coins, buttons or other small objects, which immediately disappear. It is a device that is used by all professional magicians, although they generally use a glass tumbler.

The ordinary paper cup is made into a magic one by cutting away its bottom with a knife or pair of scissors. It is a curious fact, but practically nobody ever imagines that an every-day object like a paper drinking cup might be prepared in any secret way. This is one reason for the effectiveness of the bottomless cup, as long as you do not use it more than once before the same group of people.

To make a coin or other object vanish, hold the cup in your left hand. Put a coin in the cup and cover it with a handkerchief. Then let the coin drop into the palm of your left hand. Transfer the cup and handkerchief to your right hand. Turn your right side to your audience and put the coin in a left-hand pocket. Then whisk off the handkerchief with your left hand and turn the cup upside down.

DECORATED DRINKING GLASSES. Make special drinking glasses for yourself and the rest of the family by decorating plastic drinking glasses. The glasses can be used at the dining table or for toothbrush holders. Use model airplane dope or poster paints and paint on pictures of flowers, birds and other designs, together with the name of the person to whom the glass is to be given. Decals can also be used for the decorations.

GLASS AND PAPER EXPERIMENT

GLASS AND PAPER EXPERIMENT. This is an almost unbelievable experiment. It shows how very powerful air pressure is, even though we can't feel it. Fill a glass with water and lay a piece of stiff paper on top. Hold the glass with one hand and the paper with the other, and slowly turn the glass upside down over the sink. Take your hand away from the paper. The pressure of air that pushes up against the paper is so powerful that it will keep the paper in place and the water in the glass.

INERTIA EXPERIMENT. Scientists have shown that when force is applied to move objects, they want to stay

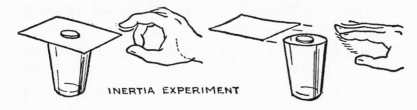

INERTIA EXPERIMENT

where they are. This wish to stay put is called inertia. If you are in a car and it suddenly starts, you fall back in your seat because of the inertia of your body.

You can show how inertia works by doing this experiment. Put a small piece of light-weight cardboard or card on top of a glass, and put a quarter on the card. Snap the card with your finger, being careful not to tilt the card upward as you snap it. The card will fly away, but the quarter, held back by its inertia, will stay behind and fall into the glass.

GLASS AND PAPER STUNT. Cut a piece of typewriter or similar paper, measuring about 3 by 6 inches. Put it on a table under a drinking glass, as shown. Ask a friend if he can move the paper out from under the glass with one finger and without moving the glass. He will probably find it impossible. Here's how: Wet the tip of your forefinger and hit down against the protruding end of the paper.

GLASS AND PAPER
STUNT

ELECTRIFIED
GLASS

THE ELECTRIFIED GLASS. This is an interesting little apparatus, which demonstrates the electrical properties of an ordinary drinking glass in quite an amazing way. First cut an arrow from a piece of stiff paper and balance it on a needle driven into a cork. Do not push the needle through the arrow. Rest the arrow on top of the needle. Cover the arrow with a glass that is perfectly dry.

If two or three of your friends are on hand, choose one of them and tell him you will make the arrow turn and point to him. Then take a piece of woolen cloth and rub the side of the glass that is toward the person chosen. That side of the glass will be electrified and the arrow will spin around to point to it. Next rub the top of the glass with the cloth, moving it in a circular direction. This will make the arrow spin around, going faster and faster until the rubbing is stopped.

CUP CATCH. Put a button in a paper cup. Jerk the cup upward so the button flies out. Then try to catch the button in the cup. Try this also with two buttons, and then three.

HOT AND COLD AIR EXPERIMENT. You can carry out a very interesting experiment with 2 glasses, a piece of blotting paper and a small piece of candle. The glasses should be the same size, and the thinner they are the better the experiment will work. First dampen the blotting paper. Then light the candle and put it in one of the glasses. Put the blotting paper on top of this glass and put the second glass, upside down, on top of the blotting paper with its rim exactly over the rim of the bottom glass. Press the upper glass down gently but firmly.

The experiment now gets under way. The candle will soon burn up all the oxygen in the bottom glass and will go out. Some of the heated air in the bottom glass will rise and escape, but as the remaining air cools, it will contract and draw the upper glass down more and more tightly against the blotting paper. A few moments after the candle goes out, you can pick up the upper glass and the bottom one will be lifted with it.

CUP BASKETS. Paper cups are easily transformed into colorful baskets for May Day, Easter or for party favors— filled with flowers, candies or nuts. Decorate them with crepe

CUP BASKETS

paper, or paper doilies, ruffles glued to the rim, with gummed stickers, rickrack, glitter and ribbon bows. Cover some cups with gold or silver paper. Add thin cardboard handles fastened with brass paper fasteners or household cement.

Bottles
and
Jars

BOTTLE GARDEN

BOTTLE BOUQUETS

WATERLESS
FISH BOWL

BOTTLE GARDENS. To make a bottle garden, use a good-sized bottle or jar which has a wide mouth. Put it on the table on its side and put in it a layer of pebbles and sand. Cover this foundation with good earth from the back yard. Wet the sand and earth before putting them in the bottle.

Now plant your garden, putting the seeds into the bottle on the end of a popsicle stick. Put grass seed in first, to make a green lawn. Then plant some orange, lemon, grapefruit or apple seeds, which will grow into little trees or bushes. Next, put in some flower seeds of any kind, or elm or maple seedlings. Plant a small piece of horseradish root to grow into a hedge.

Water your garden sparingly, taking care not to soak the

34

earth since that would rot the seeds. You can use an eye-dropper or an atomizer perfume sprayer. Punch several holes in the jar top and screw it in place. This gives the plants air, but you may sometimes have to put on a cover with no holes in it to prevent evaporation.

BOTTLE BOUQUETS. This is a method of preserving flowers and leaves in water. Use any flowers you like and make a bouquet of them by adding some sprays of green, such as cosmos leaves or asparagus fern. You can make endless combinations. Tie the stems together with thread and tie the ends of the thread around a stone. This will hold the bouquet steady in the water.

The best kind of bottle to use is a wide-mouthed one, such as a pickle bottle fitted with a screw-on lid. Put some small stones in the bottom, and lower the bouquet carefully into the bottle. Then fill the bottle with water and put on the lid.

WATERLESS FISH BOWL. Use an empty glass jar, a round one sometimes used on honey jars, if you have one. Put in the jar a little moss, some pebbles, and some air-growing greenery that needs no water. Ask your florist to help you get some of this. To the inside of one side of the bowl paste two or three colored paper fish. These may be cut from magazines or made at home, and colored with crayons or paints.

MYSTIC MOTH BALL BOTTLE. You can make some moth balls in a bottle of water rise and fall continuously without any visible means of propulsion.

Use a bottle that holds about one pint, and fill it about ¾ full of water. Add 1 tablespoon of white vinegar and then slowly, to prevent bubbling over, ½ teaspoon of bicarbonate of soda, such as ordinary baking soda. Then put 2 or 3 moth balls in the bottle, put the lid on and the gadget is ready.

The explanation of the moth balls' action is that, as they sink to the bottom, they absorb soda water. The gas bubbles in the water cling to them and soon give them enough buoyancy to force them upward. When they reach the top the gas escapes into the air. The balls then lose their buoyancy and sink again to the bottom, only to float upward again and again as the process is repeated.

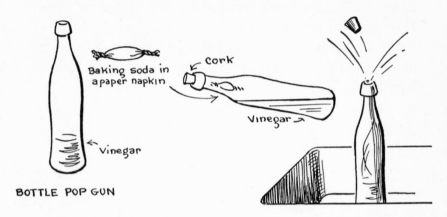

BOTTLE POP GUN

BOTTLE POP GUN. With a funnel, pour ¼ of a glass of vinegar into a bottle. Wrap 2 tablespoons of baking soda in a piece of paper napkin. Place this in the bottle. Cork the bottle at once but not too tightly and put it in the kitchen sink. In a moment or two the cork will fly out with a loud "pop."

The baking soda and vinegar make carbon dioxide gas inside the bottle. The gas presses outward with great force and soon shoots the cork out of the bottle.

BOTTLE BAROMETER. This scientific bottle barometer is a very reliable weather forecaster. Partly fill a wide-mouthed bottle with water. Turn it upside down with its mouth under more water in a saucer. As the atmospheric pressure rises and falls, the water will rise and fall inside the bottle. You can paste a scale on the outside of the bottle, if you wish. When a high pressure area, or good weather, is approaching, the water will rise on the scale. When rain, or a low pressure area is approaching, the water will fall.

BOTTLE, COIN AND TOOTHPICK STUNT. Double a wooden toothpick or match without breaking it and place it in the shape of a V over the top of a bottle. Put a coin on top of the V, as shown. The problem now is to make the coin drop into the bottle without the use of force. No one is to touch the coin, the toothpick or the bottle, and the table on which the bottle stands is not to be shaken or jolted. How can this be done?

Let a drop or two of water fall on the bent middle of the toothpick. The V will then spread out and the coin will fall into the bottle.

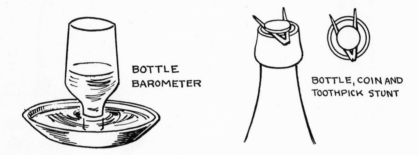

BOTTLE BAROMETER

BOTTLE, COIN AND TOOTHPICK STUNT

BOTTLE CAP PINS. To make a lapel pin, punch a hole from the inside through the center of a bottle cap with hammer and nail. Glue a circle of paper to front of cap, or coat with enamel. Then push half of a pipe cleaner through the hole and bend over the end on the front of the cap. If you paint a face on the pin, it will be the nose. Twist the other end of the pipe cleaner around a small safety pin.

Decorate the pins by painting different faces and adding yarn hair, felt or paper hats and ribbon neck bows. On some pins, use beads or buttons for eyes. Decorate others with cut-

BOTTLE CAP PINS

Yarn hair

Flower cut-out

Sequins, beads

out colored flower pictures or animal faces, coating them with clear shellac. On others, glue an ornamental button, bead or jewel in the center and surround it with beads or sequins.

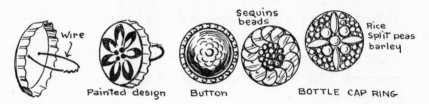

Painted design   Button   BOTTLE CAP RING

BOTTLE CAP RINGS. Make two holes in a circle of stiff cardboard. Pass wire through the holes and twist together ends of wire to make the ring fit your finger. Glue the cardboard circle inside a pop bottle cap. Then paint the cap a solid color and add a painted design or glue buttons, beads or jewels to the cap.

PILL BOTTLE FLOWER HOLDER

PILL BOTTLE FLOWER HOLDERS. Use small, clear or colored plastic pill bottles to hold fresh flowers to wear as lapel decorations. To fasten such a little bottle to your dress or suit, sew a safety pin to the center of a 14-inch length of ribbon. Tie the ribbon into a bow around the bottle, and trim the ends.

BOTTLE STATUETTES. Almost any kind of bottle can be used but try to get those that more or less resemble the human form. When beginning a statuette wash the bottle thoroughly. Then cover the entire bottle including the neck

BOTTLE
STATUETTES

with a thin covering of self-hardening clay, plasticine or home-made salt-and-flour clay. The heads are of clay or papier-mâché (bits of crepe paper mixed with glue). Noses, ears, eyebrows, beards, mustaches, locks of hair and so on, are small pieces of clay rolled between the fingers and then stuck on the clay head already in place on the bottle's neck. After pressing and shaping them with your fingers, shape and smooth them a bit finer with a spoon-type modeling tool.

The mouth, fine strands of hair, wrinkles to denote age, and other fine work can be done with a sharp pencil point. Use artificial jewels, pearls or shiny buttons for the eyes. Press them into place in the soft clay and then shape the eyelids and sockets around them. Drapes in the clothes, together with sleeves and hands, skirts and sometimes trousers, are all worked in the clay with a pencil or modeling tool and are outlined or emphasized with various colors of paint. Hats are made of clay, felt or cardboard, alone or in combination. Snipped yarn or flock can be used wherever it will add to the interest of the figure.

Lacquers or oil paints are the best coloring materials. A drawback to oils is that they take several days to dry. When a statuette is completed and painted, it should be sprayed with clear plastic.

BOTTLE CAP GARDENS. Use caps from pop bottles or the larger aluminum ones sometimes used on milk bottles.

BOTTLE CAP GARDENS

Cover inside bottom of cap with pebbles and potting soil and plant grapefruit, orange or flower seeds or very small plants. Water the garden with an eye dropper. You can also stick the stems of small artificial flowers in the soil.

MUSICAL BOTTLES

MUSICAL BOTTLES. Collect several milk and pop bottles, add a glass or two, and put different amounts of water in each. Then strike them with a spoon. The more water, the lower the pitch. Experiment with different amounts. If you make an 8-note scale, you will be able to play simple tunes.

JAR AND PAPER TRICK. It is safe to say that no one can do this stunt unless he knows the secret. Cut a piece of paper about 5 inches long by 3 inches wide. Place it flat on a table and on its center put a small milk bottle or wide-mouthed glass jar upside down. Then ask a friend to see if he can figure out a way to remove the paper without touching the bottle and without upsetting it.

The way to do this is to roll up the paper, starting at one end. Touch the sides of the paper only, so that your fingers will not touch the bottle. As you slowly roll up the paper, its rolled part will come in contact with the bottle and push it along the flat part of the paper. Soon the bottle will be pushed off the flat end of the paper, and the paper will be released without upsetting the bottle.

SNOW STORM JARS

SNOW STORM JAR. Use a round jar with a screw-on lid. With waterproof glue or household cement, fasten one or more small plastic or china figures to the inside of the lid. Let cement dry thoroughly. Then fill the jar with water almost to the top. Drop in two tablespoons of moth flakes or mica snow. Coat inside rim of lid with cement and screw it onto the jar. Let the cement dry. Then shake the jar a little and turn it upside down for a moment, and the snow will start to fall.

BOTTLE CAP FLOWERS

BOTTLE CAP FLOWERS. Cut a circle of pink, red or yellow crepe or tissue paper three times as large as a bottle cap, and scallop the edges to make petals. Remove the cork piece from the cap, put the center of the flower into the cap, put some glue on the cork, and replace the cork. Punch two holes through the cork and cap, and insert a green-covered spool wire stem. Glue beads or sequins to the cork. For a fuller flower, use two or more circles of scalloped paper.

BOTTLE PEOPLE AND ANIMALS. Bottle people can be dressed in any one of a hundred different ways. They

Ping Pong ball head

cloth head

Electric light head

Marble head

Peanut head

BOTTLE PEOPLE AND ANIMALS

are made with either bottles or jars. For the head, use some round object of the right size to fit the bottle. A tennis ball will be right for large jars, while a marble or a peanut will be right for a doll made with a small nail polish bottle. You can use ping pong balls, rubber balls, styrofoam balls, used electric light bulbs or cotton wrapped in white or pink cloth. The heads are glued to the top of the bottles.

Costumes are made from odds and ends of fabric and whatever else may be needed for hats or other details. Stuff the fabric sleeves with cotton and sew the ends closed for arms. Tie thread a short distance up the arms to make hands. Faces are painted. Use pipe cleaners for arms for small bottle people.

Animals' heads are best made, perhaps, from used electric light bulbs and bottles into which you can fit the bulbs. Cut noses and ears from colored construction paper or cloth, and complete the features and body details with poster paints and Indian ink, where needed. Use broom-straws or brush bristles for whiskers.

JAR COVER WALL DECORATIONS. Use lids that have narrow rims, and use from one to three lids for each decoration. Paint the lids black or some other color, and then paste a small, colored picture in the middle of each one. You

JAR COVER
WALL DECORATIONS

JAR COVER
COASTER

can also use snapshots of your family or friends. Glue the lids to a piece of ribbon and add a piece of ribbon tied in a bow-knot at the top.

JAR COVER COASTERS. Metal jar lids can easily be made into attractive coasters to put under glasses. Paint the jar lids black or some other color, then add a decal, a gummed sticker or a picture cut out of a magazine of a flower or some other object.

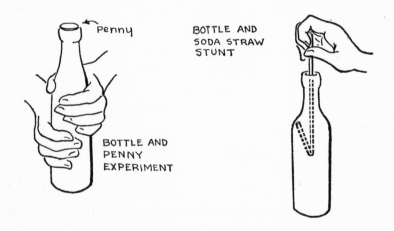

Penny

BOTTLE AND
SODA STRAW
STUNT

BOTTLE AND
PENNY
EXPERIMENT

BOTTLE AND PENNY EXPERIMENT. This experiment shows how warm air always expands and fills more space, if it can, than cold air. Put a pop bottle in the refrigerator for half an hour, to cool the air inside it. Cover a penny with a thin layer of Vaseline. Put the penny on the top of the bottle as soon as you take the bottle from the refrigerator. The Vaseline will make the penny seal the bottle top. Put both of your hands around the bottle to warm it and the air inside it. As the cold air warms up, it will expand and push in all directions. As it pushes out of the bottle, it will raise the penny.

BOTTLE AND SODA STRAW STUNT. Ask a friend if he can lift a bottle with a soda straw. Unless he knows the secret, he won't be able to. Here's how: Fold the straw and push the folded end into the bottle. You can then lift the bottle because the bent straw will jam against the shoulder of the bottle.

Vegetables and Fruits

carrot

Beet

Turnip

Apple

POTATO PEOPLE

VEGETABLE PEOPLE

POTATO PEOPLE. Select potatoes of many different shapes and sizes. The drawings show how potato people are made. Heads are fastened to bodies with toothpicks, and toothpicks can also be used for legs and arms. Wire arms and legs can also be used. Cut a cork in half lengthwise to make two feet, or use potato slices. You can also omit the feet and stick a toothpick at an angle into the back of the body. Paint features with poster paints, using thumbtacks for eyes. Potato

45

women are given skirts and blouses made from bits of cloth or crepe or tissue paper. Tie a small scarf around their necks to hide the joint between head and body.

VEGETABLE PEOPLE. These are caricature people made from a single vegetable with wire or pipe cleaner arms and legs. Carrots, beets, turnips, potatoes and apples are the best to use. Make the eyes of beads, sequins, thumbtacks or paper and the nose from a small cotton ball. The eyebrows and mouth are drawn with India ink. But the mouth may also be made of paper and cemented on. Yarn hair and hats can be added, if you wish, and also yarn mustaches. The arms and legs are stuck into the body as shown, and the feet are cemented to cardboard circles or ovals to help the odd little figures to stand up. A piece of wire or pipe cleaner or a toothpick is stuck into the back to make a prop which, together with the feet, will enable the people to stand up.

POTATO PRINTING. Designs of all kinds can be printed on paper and even cloth with an easily made potato printing press. You can make Christmas and Easter cards this way, or decorate paper napkins or letter paper. Poster paints are used when the printing is done on paper. For cloth, use textile paints, and print designs on such things as handkerchiefs, small table covers and curtains.

Use your initials or a simple design, such as a circle, triangle, cross, star or flower. Draw it on paper and cut it out. Place it on the surface of a potato cut in two lengthwise or crosswise, depending on the size of the design. With a sharp knife, cut around the outline, about ½ inch deep. Cut away all of the potato except the design, to make the design stand out in relief. Then dry the potato on a paper or cloth towel.

To print the design, cover it with paint, using a brush. Then press the design down on the paper or cloth to be decorated. Instead of brushing on paint, you can use a stamp pad, such as is used for rubber stamps, or a blotter soaked in ink or poster paint. In addition to potatoes, you can also use carrots and turnips.

POTATO PROBLEM. Ask a friend this seemingly impossible puzzle: How can you divide eleven potatoes equally among seven people? After he has figured at it long enough, tell him the answer. You make mashed potatoes and then serve equal helpings.

POTATO ANIMALS AND BIRDS. These are made like potato people. Toothpicks are used to join heads to bodies, and also for legs, ears and tails.

The elephant has paper ears and a pipe cleaner trunk. Several toothpicks are used for each leg to make them thick. The pig has a flat button nose. The horse is made with popsicle sticks. Use 2 to connect head and body and bring them out at the top for ears. Use 4 for legs. Paint features, ears and hoofs. Glue on strips of fringe for mane and tail. Cut an oval felt saddle and glue it on the horse's back. Raisins make

POTATO ANIMALS AND BIRDS

good eyes for these animals. Other animals can be made with other odd-shaped vegetables, such as sweet potatoes and carrots.

The turkey has a head cut from stiff paper or cardboard, chicken feather or pleated paper tail and wings (fasten the paper with toothpicks), matchstick legs and paper or cardboard feet.

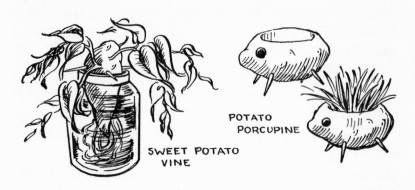

POTATO PORCUPINE

SWEET POTATO VINE

SWEET POTATO VINE. Use a sweet potato that has a few "whiskers." Put it in a jar of water, with its narrow end down. If you have one, use a jar with an opening that will support the potato. If not, stick several toothpicks into the thick end of the potato.

Put the jar in a warm, dark place, and keep it well filled with water. New roots will start to grow, and in about 10 days the stem will start to grow. As soon as this happens put the jar in a sunny window. Before long the vine will be full of green foliage.

POTATO PORCUPINE. Potato porcupines are fun for a long time, since it takes a little time for their "quills" to grow out. The porcupine's body is a well-shaped potato. Cut out some of the inside with a knife, but leave plenty of solid potato on the sides and bottom. Give the animal eyes made from thumbtacks, and legs made from matches or bits of wood.

Then plant the "quills," which are grass seeds. Fill the potato's inside with earth and scatter grass seed on it. Water every day and the grass should appear in about 10 days. You can also use moistened cotton instead of earth.

CARROT FOLIAGE. Cut off the bottom end of a carrot and hollow out its center so as to leave only a thin shell. Trim the top clean of greenery. Then hang the carrot upside down, by tying string around 2 toothpicks pushed through the carrot, as shown. Keep the carrot filled with water, and in a short time foliage will start to grow from the bottom upwards toward the light.

DISH PLANTS. This is another way to "plant" a carrot. First cut off the leaves on top, and then cut off about 2 inches of the large end of a carrot. Put this 2-inch piece, top side up, in a shallow dish or bowl. Put pebbles around it to hold it in place. Keep the pebbles moist, and new feathery leaves will soon start to grow out of the carrot's top.

You can plant the tops of beets in this same way and they will grow green and purple leaves; and you can also plant the tops of radishes and turnips.

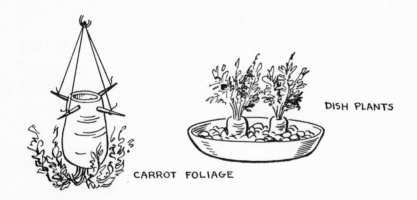

DISH PLANTS

CARROT FOLIAGE

VEGETABLE PUPPETS. Vegetables such as carrots, beets, potatoes and turnips can easily be made into puppets.

Carrots are the best for small finger puppets. All you need to do is to cut off the top 1½ inches of a carrot and then scrape out a hole in the bottom of this piece with a paring knife. Then add features. You can paint them or use India ink, or use thumbtacks, buttons or raisins for eyes, and attach

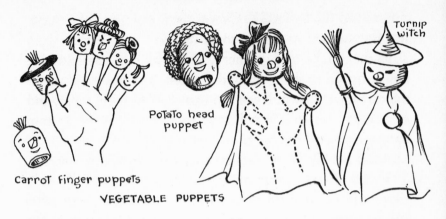

Carrot finger puppets

POTATO head puppet

Turnip witch

VEGETABLE PUPPETS

bits of carrot with pins or toothpicks for noses. Add paper, cloth or felt hats, yarn hair and any other details you can think of.

Larger puppets are made in the same way, but you make only one, which is to fit on your forefinger. Make the holes in larger vegetables such as potatoes, beets or turnips with an apple corer. For a costume, put a square of colored cloth about as big as a man's handkerchief over your hand. Then push the head on your finger. If you wish, put rubber bands around your thumb and middle finger to make hands. Amusing hair for these puppets is made by using a copper scouring pad. Remove the rivet and spread with fingers to fit the vegetable head.

CARROT AND CELERY EXPERIMENT. This will show you how plants absorb water to help them grow. Cut off the bottoms of a carrot and a piece of celery. Soak them for an hour in water, then put them in glasses containing a fairly strong solution of red ink or fabric dye. After a few hours cut the carrot in two from top to bottom, and cut across the celery. You will be able to see the red ink drawn up and absorbed by the vegetables.

LENTIL GARDENS. These gardens are like thick green forests. To make one, spread a single layer of lentil beans over a saucer. Add enough water to moisten the lentils, but not to float them. Keep the beans moist and in a sunny place, and they should sprout in about 10 days.

PLANTS FROM KITCHEN SEEDS. Watch out for and save the seeds of peppers, squash, pumpkins and other vegetables. When you collect these, spread them out to dry on a paper towel. Then plant them in small flower pots or in round waxed boxes, like those that are used for cottage cheese. Punch holes in the bottoms of the boxes for drainage.

To fill flower pots properly, cover the bottom with pebbles or pieces of broken flower pots. Then fill with good soil to within ½ inch of the top. If the soil where you live is poor, you can get small bags of good soil or humus at ten-cent stores. Florists also have good soil. Put your flower pots in a sunny window and water them daily, and your seeds will soon sprout and grow.

OAT GARDENS. You will need some oat seeds and a foil pie tin. First cover the bottom of the tin with small stones for drainage. Put a layer of earth over the stones, and then a layer of oat seeds. Cover the seeds lightly with fine soil. Then cover the pie tin with a thin cloth, put it in a sunny window, and sprinkle it with water every day. The oats should begin to come up about the third day. When they do, remove the cloth and watch the feathery plants grow.

For another good garden, cover the bottom of a pie tin with a sheet of cotton and put seeds such as beans or squash on the cotton. Keep the cotton moist and the seeds will sprout.

PLANTS FROM KITCHEN SEEDS

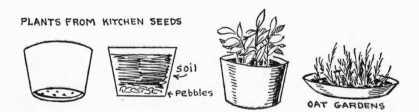

soil

← Pebbles

OAT GARDENS

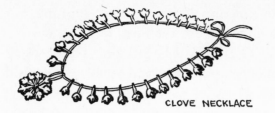

CLOVE NECKLACE

Pendant

CLOVE NECKLACES. These necklaces give off a wonderful spicy perfume. Use red, black or green string. Cut the string to the length you want the necklace to be, put it on waxed paper in a curve, and then attach the cloves to the string with quick-drying model airplane glue or a similar glue or cement.

Put the stem end of a clove on the glue, and hold the clove there until the glue hardens. Continue to add cloves, ½ inch apart, until the necklace is completed. After the first glue has dried, drop an additional bit of glue on the stem of each clove. Make a pendant of eight cloves pasted to a small cardboard disk. Tie the pendant to the center of the necklace.

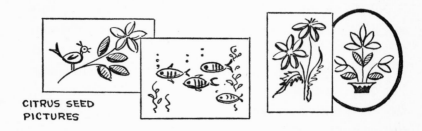

CITRUS SEED PICTURES

CITRUS SEED PICTURES. Orange seeds are shaped so as to be perfect for the bodies of birds. Lemon seeds are excellent for flower petals and leaves, while grapefruit seeds are good for ducks and fish. Keep each kind of seed in a separate envelope or box. When ready to use them, split them in half, glue the flat sides to a card, and paint them. Thus, for example, one orange seed will make two birds. Add details needed to complete a picture with paints and India ink. For bird pictures, draw branches for the birds to perch on.

MELON AND VEGETABLE SEEDS. The seeds of watermelons, cantaloupes, pumpkins and squash can be used for making jewelry and seed pictures and for decorating boxes. Seeds that are light in color can be dyed with household dyes.

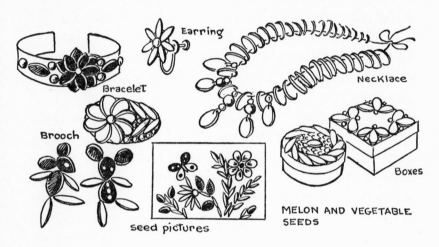

Earring

Bracelet

Necklace

Brooch

seed pictures

Boxes

MELON AND VEGETABLE SEEDS

Necklaces and bracelets can be made by stringing these seeds in different ways on linen thread. The drawings show a few examples. If the seeds are dry and difficult to push a needle through, soak them in warm water for a few hours. For different effects, combine the seeds with beads in necklaces and bracelets. When making flower earrings, arrange the seeds on the earring backs with tweezers.

For pictures, these seeds are good for flowers, trees, birds and fishes. Use dyed seeds, and paint undyed seeds with poster paints. For box decorations, the seeds can be arranged in many different ways. The drawings show a few examples.

ORANGE AND APPLE POMANDERS. These sachets have a delightful aroma. Put them in drawers or tie ribbons to them and hang them up in closets. To make one, push cloves into an orange or apple until the surface is completely covered. This makes a pomander which will continue to give off its spicy scent for a long time.

MINIATURE FRUIT ORCHARDS. The seeds of almost any common fruit, such as apples, oranges, grapefruit or pears, can be grown by putting them between two layers of moist paper towels. Keep the towels moist for three or four weeks, and sprouts will begin to appear. When this happens, put the sprouts in a coffee can filled with earth, and you will soon have a miniature orchard full of greenery.

Cardboard
and
Tin Containers

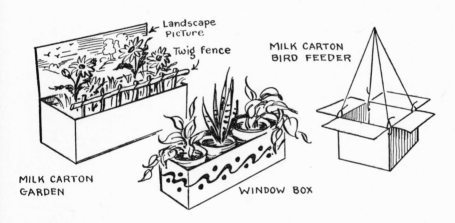

MILK CARTON GARDEN. Cut along both ends and a side of one side of a milk carton. Raise this side to form a background, and paste a landscape picture on it. Paint the rest of the carton green, brown or red. Fill it with a mixture of soil and peat moss, and put twigs into the soil in the foreground to make a fence. Stick artificial flowers into the soil in some places, and sprinkle grass seed to grow in other places. Add some stones here and there, and possibly a pocket mirror pool, and some miniature figures, bridges and pagodas. Fairy-like shrubbery can be added by gilding and painting weeds and sticking them into the soil.

WINDOW BOX. Cut away one side of a milk carton and paint the part that is left with poster paints or house paint. Then use the box to hold potted plants or partly fill them with soil and plant flower and other seeds in them.

MILK CARTON BIRD FEEDER. Use a 1- or 2-quart milk carton. Cut off the upper part so as to leave the bottom 4 inches high. Slit the 4 corners down for 1 inch from the top and bend back the 4 flaps so the birds can perch on them. Paint the carton green or brown. Make holes at each corner for wire or string and hang the feeder from a tree branch. Foods to put in the feeder include bread crumbs, popcorn, rolled oats, raisins, small seed mixtures, corn meal and bits of apples and other fresh and dried fruits.

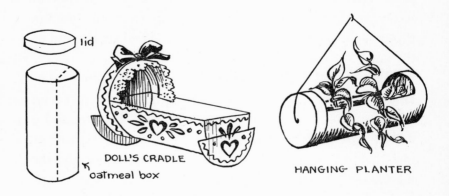

lid

DOLL'S CRADLE

oatmeal box

HANGING PLANTER

DOLL'S CRADLE. Cut away most of one side of an oatmeal box. Then glue it to the lid as shown. Glue on 2 cardboard rockers, and paint with poster paints.

HANGING PLANTER. Cut an oatmeal box to the shape shown, and paint it green with poster paints. Make holes in each end and thread wire or strong cord through them for hanging.

COFFEE CAN FEEDER. This is an excellent bird feeder to hang from the branch of a tree, where it will be safe from cats. Punch a hole in the center of the top and bottom

of a coffee can or any other can that has a removable lid. Next, punch holes in the centers of 2 pie tins or heavy foil pans. Then tie a knot in the end of a piece of clothesline or heavy cord. Thread the clothesline up from the bottom through the pie tins and the coffee can. Then tie the end of the cord to a tree branch.

STRING HOLDERS. Every kitchen needs a handy container for string. Here are two that can be made very easily.

For one, use a small tin about 4 inches in diameter and 4 inches high, with a removable lid. With rubber cement or glue, fasten blue or red checked material to the box and the lid. Or use gift wrapping paper, wall paper or colorful cretonne. Make a small hole in the center of the lid with an ice pick or nail. Put a ball of string in the box, and bring its end through the hole.

Use a 1-pint ice cream container for another string holder. Punch a hole in the center of the lid. Paste a paper reinforcement ring around the hole on the inside. Decorate the container by pasting on cut-out colored pictures, applying decals, or using one of the methods given above for the tin can string holder.

KITCHEN DRUM. You can make excellent drums by covering the open ends of coffee cans, large oatmeal boxes or salt boxes with wrapping paper. To make drums that have a louder, deeper sound, use two thicknesses of wrapping paper. Use pencils or sticks with spools on the end for drumsticks.

TIN CAN GARDEN BOOKENDS. These are attractive bookends made from coffee cans or other cans with lids that don't have to be cut open with a can opener. You need two similar cans to make a pair of bookends. Give the outsides of the cans a coat of quick-drying enamel. Then decorate them by gluing on colored cut-out pictures, applying decals or by tracing or stenciling designs on them. When the decorations are completed, fill the cans with a mixture of soil and peat moss and plant ivy or other plants in them.

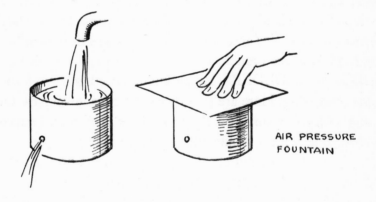

AIR PRESSURE FOUNTAIN

AIR PRESSURE FOUNTAIN. This is an experiment that shows how we are surrounded at all times by air pressure that is stronger than we realize. Punch a hole in the side of an empty coffee can by hammering a nail through it. Hold the can over the sink and fill it with water. The air pressure will push down and force the water out of the hole in the can. Now lay a piece of cardboard over the top of the can and press it down a little. The cardboard will block the air pressure and the fountain will stop.

RACING WHEEL. A tin can racing wheel is easy to make from the removable top of a tin can. Punch a hole

RACING WHEEL

through its center with a nail. Then pass a piece of string about a yard long through the hole and tie a large knot in its outer end. This completes the racer, which is shown in the drawing.

To race with the wheel, hold the free end of the string in your hand and start to run. At first the wheel will lag behind. Then it will catch up with you and pass you. As you increase your speed, you will once more get ahead of the wheel, but then, if you do not watch out, it will pick up speed and get ahead of you. It is a good toy and will race with you as long as your breath holds out.

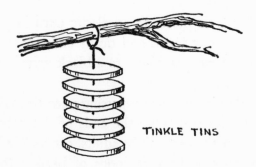

TINKLE TINS

TINKLE TINS. Punch holes in the centers of 6 tops from tin cans such as coffee cans that have a removable lid. Run string or cord through the holes and knot the string so the lids are about ½ inch apart. Hang them in the wind and they will make a musical tinkle, like oriental chimes.

ICE CREAM CARTON JEWELRY. This jewelry is made from the lids of plastic ice cream cartons. The plastic is prepared by rubbing it with medium sandpaper, which rubs off the lettering and gives the plastic an attractive frosted appearance.

ICE CREAM CARTON JEWELRY

Cut off the rim of the carton. Then cut circles, diamonds, ovals and other shapes from the top. Color the thin edges of the pieces with crayons, or coat them with glue and dip in glitter. To make a necklace, punch holes in the tops of the pieces and tie them with thread to a length of ribbon, yarn or colored cord. Tie two or more pieces together to serve as necklace pendants.

For bracelets, tie pieces to an elastic cord loop. Measure the cord to fit your wrist, and tie its ends together with a square knot. Or cement pieces to a black velvet ribbon fastened with a snap.

Make children's earrings by passing yarn through holes in the tops of pieces and tying the ends of the yarn to make loops to fit over the ears. Make adults' earrings by fastening pieces to earring backs with loops of bead wire or yarn. Cement the top ends of the loops to the discs on earring backs.

TIN CAN STILTS. Use 2 large fruit juice cans. Punch 2 holes opposite each other in each can near the closed end. Do this with a hammer and nail. Get 2 pieces of clothesline or other similar rope, each 6 feet long. Put the ropes through the holes in the cans and tie knots on their ends. Paint the cans, if you wish.

To walk on the stilts, step onto the cans and hold the ropes in your hands. When you lift your feet, pull on the ropes to keep the cans against your feet.

BULL ROARER. Some people call these devices Bull Roarers, rosin cans or squawkers. They give off a loud roaring sound. Take a medium-size tin can that has a replaceable cover. Remove the cover, and make a small hole in the bottom. Thread through this hole a piece of heavy string well rubbed with rosin. You can get rosin at music stores, which keep it on hand for violinists. Tie a knot in each end of the string and everything is all set.

Hold the can with your left hand, clipping the string between your left fingers. Then take the other end of the string in your right hand, pull it taut and pull it through the hole, letting the string slip slowly through your left fingers.

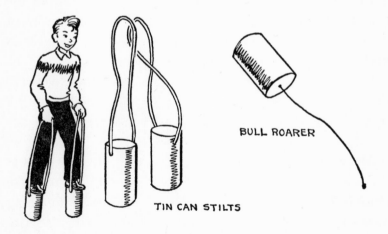

BULL ROARER

TIN CAN STILTS

FLOWER VASES. Use small cans, such as those in which frozen orange juice comes. Remove the top of the can. Then paint it black or some other color, using poster paints. When the paint has dried, add a leaf or floral border at top and

FLOWER VASE

IVY PLANTER
AND TRELLIS

bottom. Then paint a floral design on the side of the tin or decorate with a decal. Apply a coat of shellac to add brilliance.

IVY PLANTER AND TRELLIS. Use a rectangular tin such as those in which some canned meats are packed. With rubber cement, fasten a strip of flowered cretonne around the tin. Then make a little trellis by gluing together 4 popsicle sticks or round sticks from candy suckers. Give the trellis one or more coats of white paint or enamel. Plant the ivy in good soil, and stick the trellis into the soil.

CHEESE BOX TOMTOM

Lid

STATIONERY
HOLDER

CHEESE BOX TOM-TOM. This Indian tom-tom is made from one of the round cardboard boxes in which many kinds of cheese are packed. With a sharp-pointed knife, cut away almost half of the cover. Then get a piece of heavy string and tie a small stick, about 3 inches long, to its center. The string is then passed around the outside of the box and tied tightly underneath the bottom. Half of the stick will now rest on the cover, and the other half will project over the open part of the box. When you tap on the free end of the stick, the beat will sound like the hollow throb of a real Indian tom-tom.

STATIONERY HOLDER. This is a good-looking box that can be used as a stationery holder, a recipe file, or for any other household purpose. It is made from a paper napkin box. Remove one end and cut off the upper half of the front. Then cut the two sides on a slant from the front up to the top of the back. Paste attractive wallpaper to all parts, or paint and decorate with poster paints. Decals and gummed stickers can also be used for decorations.

EGG CARTON FLOWERS

EGG CARTON FLOWERS. To make tulips, cut out the soft paper cup-shaped sections of egg cartons, trim the edges with scissors to make petals, and paint them with poster paints. Push a wire or pipe cleaner stem through a hole in the bottom of each flower. Bend its top over and glue it in place. Add green paper leaves.

If you flatten one of these tulips and paint it purple with a yellow center, it will look like a pansy.

PICTURE PUZZLES. Cut off one side of a large rectangular cereal box for each puzzle. Coat the printed side with glue and put a colored magazine picture on the glue, smoothing it to prevent wrinkles. Cut the cardboard into irregularly shaped pieces and the picture puzzle is made and ready to use. Keep the puzzle in a box or large envelope so the pieces will not get lost.

BEAN RATTLES (MARACAS). A home-made bean rattle makes a noise like those in Cuban and Mexican orchestras. You can use your own maraca to keep time with the music you hear on the radio or TV. Use any medium-size tin can that has a replaceable cover. Put a handful of dried beans, rice and pebbles in the can, put on the cover, and fasten it down with adhesive tape. Then shake the can and it will make the rattling noise characteristic of the maraca.

Eggs
and
Egg Shells

EGG SHELL
GARDENS

EGG SHELL
FLOWER BOWLS

EGG SHELL GARDENS. When eggs are being broken for cooking, ask that they be broken near the pointed end. Then use the rest of the shell—the lower part—for the flower holder. Wash the shells, and then color them. A good way to do this is to pour about 1 inch of enamel into a small round-bottomed bowl and then turn the shell around and around in the bowl. This will paint it inside and out and make it more durable. Give each shell 2 coats of the enamel. Then place it on a clean dish to dry. The shells can also be colored with household fabric dyes or Easter egg dyes. It is best to color the shells in soft pastel colors.

You can plant the shells with live flowers and plants, with dried flowers, grasses and weeds or with artificial flowers. For live flowers, fill a shell with soil, crush the bottom a little for drainage, and stand the shell up on a saucer. To hold it upright, support it with a ring of paper coated with cement, or with clay or kneaded bread. Plant small flower seeds or lemon, orange or apple seeds. Do not plant them deep. Just press them into the top of the soil. Keep the gardens in a sunny window and water them every day.

If you fill your garden with dried flowers, use such things as straw flowers, red starflowers, grasses and weeds painted gold, silver and other colors. Fill the egg shell with sand or soil, and stick the stems of the plants into it. Follow the same procedure with artificial flowers.

EGG SHELL FLOWER BOWLS. These bowls are made in much the same way as Egg Shell Gardens, but the hole in the shell is on one side instead of in one end. To make the opening, tap the side of an egg lightly on a water faucet, and then carefully pick the shell from the tapped area. Empty the shell, wash it out, and turn it upside down to dry.

Color the shell in pastel shades of enamel, applying two coats. Then fill the shell with sand or soil and "plant" live, dried or artificial flowers and plants.

EGG SHELL GLITTER

EGG SHELL GLITTER. Egg shell glitter is made by breaking egg shells into very small pieces. Break the shells with your fingers, and then crush the pieces by rolling them with a rolling pin. Use dyed shells or paint with poster paints before breaking them. You can also use plain shells and paint the glitter after it has been put on an object.

Use the glitter to decorate boxes, bottles and tin cans. Coat the entire surface you are going to decorate with glue. Then sprinkle vari-colored glitter on it, or roll the object in glitter. When the glue has dried, apply a coat of shellac or clear "dope."

Decorate small pill bottles to use as bud vases, typewriter ribbon boxes and cardboard boxes to use as pin boxes or odds and ends containers, small frozen fruit juice tins to use as flower vases, and nut cups for use at parties. You can also draw stars, butterflies, birds, simple flowers and other objects on the lids of small boxes of every kind, coat the designs with glue, and sprinkle the glue with vari-colored glitter. Wherever it may be needed, use India ink to divide different parts of a design or to mark in needed details.

EGG SHELL JEWELRY

EGG SHELL JEWELRY. Egg shell jewelry is made by gluing egg shell glitter to different forms of cardboard shapes. When jewelry pieces made with colored glitter are completed, they are coated with clear nail polish to give them sparkle. Uncolored glitter can be painted with metallic paint or enamel. Gold and copper enamel make particularly good-looking effects. Finished jewelry pieces can be further decorated with beads, pearls, rhinestones, shells, small artificial flowers or macaroni letters.

When making a jewelry piece, coat the surface of the cardboard shape with cement and sprinkle it with the glitter. It is often best to stiffen the cardboard shapes by gluing two of them together. The shapes may be circles, ovals, squares, diamonds or any other shape you wish to use. The drawings show examples of egg shell bracelets, necklaces, lapel pins and earrings.

EGG SHELL TULIPS

EGG SHELL ANIMALS AND BIRDS

EGG SHELL TULIPS. Crack the large end of a raw egg and remove enough shell so the contents can be poured out. Then, using sharp nail scissors, cut the shell to tulip shape. Make small cuts to minimize the danger of cracking the shell.

Punch a hole in the bottom, from the inside, with a needle or pin. Wire an artificial tulip center or some fringed black crepe or tissue paper to a wire or pipe cleaner stem. Put the stem through the hole in the shell and secure it with cement. Wind green crepe or tissue paper around the stem just below the shell, and then wind the paper around the stem, adding paper leaves as you do so. Use dyed shells or paint the shells with poster paints. The shells can be dipped in melted paraffin to make them more durable.

EGG SHELL ANIMALS AND BIRDS. These can be made with hard-boiled eggs or with eggs from which the insides have been blown out. If you use blown eggs, save the eggs to scramble and then use the shell for making egg animals.

The giraffe is made with an egg painted or dyed yellow

with brown spots painted on it. Make the neck and head from 2 pieces of paper. Paste them together except for 1 inch at the bottom. Paste bottom ends to each side of egg. Add a string tail and toothpick legs.

The egg for the penguin's body is painted black except for the front. Cut 2 black paper circles for the head. The eyes are 2 notebook reinforcement rings, and the beak is a small piece of yellow paper. Paste the bottom of one circle to front of egg and of other circle to the back. Then paste the rest of the circles together. Cut feet from black paper or cardboard colored black with India ink. Add a red paper bow tie.

The drawings show how other animals or animal heads are made and are placed on nut cups to hold them upright.

THE OBEDIENT EGG. Show this mystifying stunt to your friends. Fill a jar or pitcher with salt water made with lots of salt. The salt water is so buoyant that an egg will float in it instead of sinking to the bottom, as in fresh water. Put an egg in the water and say, "Rise up, O egg!" The egg will sink a little way and will then obediently rise to the surface.

HOW TO PRINT PICTURES ON EGGS. This is a little-known way to transfer pictures from newspapers onto eggs. You can use pictures from the comics or from colored advertisements. First hard-boil some eggs. Then cut out the pictures you want to print on them. They must, of course, be small enough to fit on an egg. Hold an egg in your left hand, and rub wax paraffin on the side where you are going to put the picture. Keep adding paraffin until the side is well coated. Then put the picture face down on the waxed part, and rub with the curved bottom of a spoon. When you remove the paper, the picture will be printed on the egg.

EGGHEADS. The eggheads are made of hard-boiled eggs or blown eggs. Many people also use the thin china hollow eggs that are used to encourage hens to lay. These are inexpensive and are sold by most hardware stores. The finished egghead people are used for party favors, prizes, gifts and decorations.

Characters of all kinds can be made. A scientist with black paper eyeglasses; an artist with a beret, a goatee and a palette; a chef with a chef's cap; an Indian with a paper feather head-dress; a baby with a bonnet made of lace doilies with bows of pink or blue ribbon; flappers with fancy hair and flowered hats; clowns, cowboys, Santa Claus, Easter bunnies and so on. Some people make collections of eggheads of famous people of all kinds—actors, statesmen and so on.

Faces are made in several different ways. One way is to pencil in the features, copying pictures that have different expressions. Then use blue enamel for the eyes, fingernail polish for the mouth and leave the eyebrows and nose in pencil. Add yarn for hair, strand by strand, and ears of paper. A tiny ball of cotton can sometimes be used for a nose.

Another way to make the faces is to pencil in the features and then paint them with a very fine brush and poster paints. Put two dabs of pink paint for the top of the cheek bones. Just above them outline the eyes with black paint, fill in the outlined part with white, then do the iris, either blue or brown, and add a dot of black for the pupil. Eyelashes and eyebrows are added next, and a couple of red strokes for nostrils and lips.

Instead of using yarn for the hair, try goat's hair which is used for making doll's hair. You can get it at a doll hospital that mends broken dolls.

Women's hats are made in infinite variety of felt, crepe paper, cloth, lace, artificial flowers, feathers, ribbons and so on. One good way to make hats is to use the cup-like parts of soft paper egg cartons. Remove these and paint them in different colors. While they are still wet from the paint, shape them into different styles.

Eggheads are mounted on several different kinds of bodies or stands. One way is to glue them into the top of a towel

Tube body

Paper cup body

Pipe cleaner body

Felt

Paper collar

Wire coil

Papier mâché or clay base.

EGG HEADS

roll or mailing tube body. The body is then dressed in clothes made of tissue paper, crepe paper or cloth. Arms are made by passing long pipe cleaners (hobby shop) through holes in the sides of the tube. Glue them in place where they enter the holes. Then glue cardboard feet to the bottom of the tube.

Another method of finishing and mounting is to give the eggheads small-sized pipe cleaner bodies. Put a pipe cleaner through the bottom hole in the shell to make the body. Wind another cleaner around it to make it stronger and to keep the head in place. Wind a third cleaner once around the "neck" and let the ends extend as arms. Tie a ribbon bow around the neck. Leave the body as it is, or dress it in any way you wish.

Eggheads of this kind are sometimes glued to one side of small cardboard boxes. Cover the boxes with decorative paper and bind the edges with adhesive tape. On the box put small reproductions of things that the character shown would use.

Other methods of mounting include the use of a round construction paper collar made by cutting a piece of paper 6 inches long and ¾ inch wide and gluing or taping the ends together; gluing the shell to an upside-down nut cup, or gluing the shell to a cone-shaped paper cup with its pointed end cut off. You can also mount an egghead on a small block of styrofoam in which a slight depression has been made, on a coil made of medium heavy wire and on a clay or papier-mâché pedestal base like the one shown in the drawing.

EGG SHELL
FLOWER
PAINTING

EGG SHELL
MOSAIC PICTURES

EGG SHELL FLOWER PAINTINGS. This is a hobby for those who have a good deal of patience and are willing to work slowly and carefully.

Use shells from hard boiled eggs, and use as models the seed catalog pictures of such flowers as rosebuds, pansies, dogwood, cosmos and poppies. The shells are carefully broken or cut into shapes and sizes to represent petals and flowers. The pieces are then picked up with tweezers and cemented to a penciled outline design drawn on cardboard. Stems are made of green cord, and vases to hold the flowers are made from crushed egg shells coated with clear nail polish. When a picture is completed, it is tinted with water colors and mounted in a frame, preferably a shadow frame.

EGG SHELL MOSAIC PICTURES. Mosaic pictures and designs are made by fitting together small ceramic or plastic pieces. The same effects can be achieved by breaking dyed shells or shells colored with poster paints or enamel into small pieces, and arranging the pieces to make a mosaic picture. When you break the shells, keep the different colors separate in different boxes. The shell pieces used for mosaic work are much larger than those in egg shell glitter. That is what makes the difference between mosaic pictures and decorating with egg shell glitter.

Make a design, or find one, that is very simple and has well-defined areas of different colors. Draw the design in pencil on a paper plate or a piece of colored construction paper. Then, using tweezers, apply the egg shell pieces one at a time, with the colored side up. Put a dab of glue on each piece before you put it in place. Work from the center of the design out, and finish one color area at a time. Do the background areas last.

You can also make the mosaics by coating the color areas one at a time with glue, and putting the egg shell pieces on the glue before it hardens. In addition, you can use undyed shells. Fill in one color area at a time and paint the shell pieces before going on to the next color area.

EGG SHELL GLOW LIGHTS

EGG SHELL GLOW LIGHTS. These lights give off a lovely soft glow. To make one, punch about 12 holes in the sides of a raw egg. Use a large needle and tap its end gently with a spoon or some other object. When these holes have been made, make 1-inch holes at the top and bottom and blow out the egg's contents.

Make a base for the light by putting a circle of clay or kneaded bread in a small metal jar lid, and turn up the edges of the clay. Stick a large size cake candle in the center of the clay. Put the egg shell over the candle, resting it on the turned up edges of the clay, as shown. This will leave air spaces that will enable the candle to burn.

PAINTED EGGS

PAINTED EGGS. Pictures of many different kinds can be painted on eggs, both for Easter and for year-round gifts. As with the Eggheads, you can use blown eggs, hard boiled eggs or the thin china artificial eggs, all of which can be painted with enamels or poster paints. A very fine brush is needed because the working space is small. The pictures are usually on one side of the egg only.

The pictures that can be used are of all kinds and are of the types found in magazines, newspapers and greeting cards. If you are not able to draw them freehand, you can start by tracing them on eggs with carbon paper. It is probable that before long you will be able to draw simple pictures on the eggs and will not have to trace.

Pictures that can be used include bunnies sitting under a flower, simple flower bouquets, flying bluebirds, ducklings swimming in a pond, Mother Goose characters and so on.

Another way to paint eggs is to use small and colorful decorative designs and to cover the entire egg with them. This has been a custom for many centuries in Czechoslovakia. Experts at this craft first hold an egg in their left hand and draw the designs on it in pencil, using a book as a support to steady the right hand. The pattern is gone over with a pen and India ink, and is then painted with water colors. When the paint is dry, the egg is given a coat of shellac or clear nail polish. The drawings give an indication of how these eggs look when completed. But they cannot show the infinite number of different designs that can be made. American Indian designs, flowers, birds, hearts and dozens of other pictures and designs that you can find in magazines, greeting cards, design books and so on, can be used.

ENGRAVING YOUR NAME ON AN EGG. You and your friends can "engrave" your names in bold relief on hardboiled eggs. First write or print your name or initials on an egg with a piece of beeswax. You can get beeswax at a department store or ten-cent store. When you have written your name, put the egg in a bowl of vinegar. The acid in the vinegar will eat away the shell wherever it is not covered with beeswax and in two or three hours your name will be engraved on the egg.

A
Kitchen
Miscellany

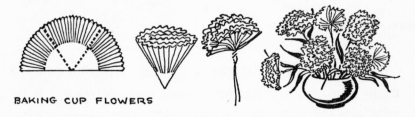

BAKING CUP FLOWERS

BAKING CUP FLOWERS. Use colored baking cups. Fold one in half, and then in thirds, as shown. Put your fingers in the ruffles and twist to form the flower. Cement or glue the flower to a pipe cleaner or wire stem. Wind green-covered spool wire around the base of the flower. Add paper or ready-made leaves. Wear a flower as a lapel decoration, or make a number of flowers and put them in a vase.

DIVING RAISINS. Fill a glass with soda pop, and drop five raisins into it. The raisins will sink to the bottom. But keep watching and you will see them rise to the top. Watch a little longer and they will again sink down. It is the action of the gas in the carbonated pop that makes the raisins rise and fall. Use a light-colored drink so that you can see the raisins clearly.

STARCH DETECTOR. This is a simple method of finding out if different foods contain starch. The starch detector is a medicine dropper filled with tincture of iodine. Test potatoes, white and whole wheat bread, flour, sugar, vegetables and any other foods. If the food is cooked, moisten it with water. Boil any uncooked food, such as potatoes or rice, for a few minutes. This will release the starch. Put one or two drops of iodine on the food. If the iodine, which is brown, turns to dark blue, it means that the food contains starch.

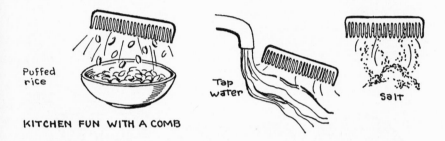

Puffed rice

Tap water

Salt

KITCHEN FUN WITH A COMB

KITCHEN FUN WITH A COMB. These are experiments in which you charge a comb with electricity. It is what the scientists call frictional electricity, or electricity made by rubbing.

Rub a hard rubber comb hard and fast on a woolen coat sleeve. Then dip it into a bowl of puffed rice. Pull the comb out and hold it over a table. The rice will stick to the comb and then will jump off in all directions.

Rub a comb as before and hold it near water running out of a tap of the sink. Watch the water bend toward the comb, attracted by the electricity.

Make a small pile of salt on a table, and hold an electrified comb one inch above it. The salt will jump up and stick fast to the comb.

These experiments work best on a clear, cold day.

ALUMINUM FOIL FLOWERS. Cut five strips of foil, each 4 inches long by 2 inches wide. Roll each strip around a thick pencil, and then tie in the middle with spool wire,

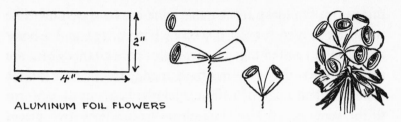

ALUMINUM FOIL FLOWERS

leaving a double strand of wire for the stem. Fold together the two parts on each side of the middle to make two flowers. Group all ten flowers together to make a corsage or nosegay. Tie the stems with a ribbon bow.

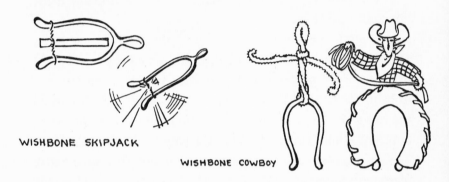

WISHBONE SKIPJACK

WISHBONE COWBOY

WISHBONE SKIPJACKS. Let a wishbone dry out for a day or two. Then take a piece of string, double it, and tie it to the wishbone as shown. Take a wooden match or other small stick of wood, which is a little shorter than the wishbone, cut a couple of notches in it about ½ inch from one end, and put this end between the double string. Using the match as a lever, twist the string round and round until it is tightly wound up. Then pull the match up toward the head of the wishbone until the string slips into the notches and holds it tight.

To make the skipjack perform, place it on a table with the long end of the match or stick underneath, as in the drawing. The moment you let go of the match, the wishbone will spring into the air, making a leap of several feet.

WISHBONE COWBOYS. One of the most amusing

things you can make from a wishbone is a cowboy doll. The wishbone is used for the cowboy's bowed legs, and a body and head of twisted pipe cleaners, plus pipe cleaner arms, are added. When the body has been made, dress it in a bright plaid shirt and a pair of yellow oilcloth chaps cut to conform to the bow-legged legs. The chaps are made of two pieces of oilcloth laced together around the edges with brown woolen yarn. A ten-gallon hat is made of the oilcloth or of felt or paper. Bend the arms into position to hold a lariat of narrow leather lacing arranged as shown.

WISHBONE GOOD LUCK PINS. You can make yourself a good-luck pin.

One pin is made by washing a wishbone, sanding it smooth, and then painting it. You can use gold or copper paint or bright-colored poster paints. Another way to decorate it is to paint the head only, and then wind colored ribbon around the rest of it. Tie a ribbon bow around the neck of the wishbone and stick a small safety pin through the back of the bow.

You can also cement a painted wishbone to a cardboard, plastic, plywood or wallboard circle. Cement a pinback to the back of the circle or cement the circle to a felt circle with a safety pin sewed to it.

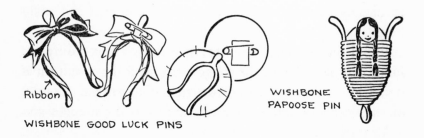

Ribbon

WISHBONE GOOD LUCK PINS

WISHBONE
PAPOOSE PIN

WISHBONE PAPOOSE PIN. Clean a wishbone well, and coat it with transparent nail polish. The wishbone is the papoose's cradle board. Use a small acorn for the papoose's head. Push a toothpick into its small end to be the body. Sew or cement a small piece of cardboard to back of the wishbone. Lay the "papoose" on it and, with a needle, weave yarn back and forth over the "body." Glue braids of black yarn to the acorn head for hair and put in the features with India ink. To use the papoose as a lapel pin, insert a small safety pin through the yarn at the back.

TOWEL ROLL NAPKIN RINGS

TOWEL ROLL BAZOOKA

TOWEL ROLL NAPKIN RINGS. Cut 2-inch-wide sections from a towel roll for each napkin ring. Decorate them by wrapping with colored yarn or cord, or by pasting on silver paper, wallpaper or decorative gift wrap paper.

TOWEL ROLL BAZOOKA. A bazooka like this one makes a very fascinating noise when you hum a tune into its open end. Take the roll from a used roll of paper towels, and punch four or five holes along one side. Then put a piece of wax paper over one end and fasten it in place with adhesive tape. Hum or sing a tune into the opposite end. The notes will vibrate against the wax paper and make a loud humming sound.

PIE TIN GARDENS. Arrangements of many different kinds can be made, as the suggestions given here will show you. Chinese and Japanese gardens are among the most popular, so details are given here of the materials used in them.

Use a foil pie tin. Fill it about two thirds full of soil or papier-mâché. Whichever you use, sprinkle green glitter over it or, for a more exotic effect, gold glitter. Put a small mirror in the center to form a lake, and put colored pebbles around the edge of the lake. At one end put a small ten-cent-store Japanese paper parasol. Then "plant" tiny colored strawflowers to make a flower garden. (Get these from a florist.) In each garden put one of the small Chinese or Japanese figures of a man or woman and also of a temple or pagoda, which are sold by some ten-cent stores, gift shops and florists. They are always available, but you may have to look around a little to find the shops that sell them. Make tiny rickshaws of cardboard, with toothpick shafts and button wheels. Paint them with water colors or poster paints. Make miniature Ming trees with wire trunks and green rubber sponge foliage.

Many other materials can be used in both Chinese and other gardens. Draw and color small figures or cut them from

PIE TIN GARDENS

magazines or greeting cards. Glue these to thin wires or broken toothpicks that can be stuck into the soil or other base material. A little girl with a watering can, a boy with a big straw hat, fairies with silver wings, butterflies and dozens of other figures can be used.

Use twigs for tree trunks, adding rubber sponge foliage. Tiny artificial rose leaves also make excellent foliage. Use dyed weeds for bushes, and also bits of natural sponge colored with tempera paints or vegetable coloring. Use green cellulose sponge for hedges. Paint pieces of tapioca orange to look like oranges, and put them on some of the trees. Use small beads of all colors to represent fruit on trees. Cement tiny colored plastic birds to some trees. These are available at most ten-cent stores. Miniature bridges are most easily made of paper or lightweight cardboard, though clay is also used. Small, flat stones make pathways. Tiny garden seats and wishing wells are made of paper or lightweight cardboard. Small plastic bottle caps make urns that can hold flowers or sponge greenery. Tiny plastic animals can be placed here and there.

The charm bracelet figures of people, buildings, windmills and many other things can often be used, as can tiny artificial flowers. Small sticks and bits of wood are used for logs and glued together to make fences. Sand can be glued around the edge of mirror lakes. Flat seeds can be arranged as borders around a garden, giving it a trim and attractive finish. There is really no end to the possibilities when your imagination once gets to work on these miniature gardens.

STOVE MAT
KITCHEN PLAQUES

STOVE MAT KITCHEN PLAQUES. These are made from a common kitchen article, a ten-cent asbestos stove mat. To make a plaque, paint the smooth side of a mat with a light pastel enamel. Then glue a good-looking picture of any interesting kind to the mat. Finish by painting the rim of the mat with a bright-colored enamel that goes well with the pastel color and the picture. If you wish, cover the front of the finished mat with cellophane, overlapping the edge and taped to the back.

FUN WITH BREAD. Did it ever occur to you that ordinary bread is a good deal like modeling clay? It is, as a matter of fact, for it is pliable and can easily be modeled into any simple shape. The method of making things from bread is the same as for clay, but with bread there are two important rules. First, it must be white bread to give clean, clear colors; and second, it must be fresh. If you do not use all of it at one time, wrap it up in a damp cloth.

Things you can make of bread are beads, flowers, animals and birds. Bread flowers can be arranged on large buttons

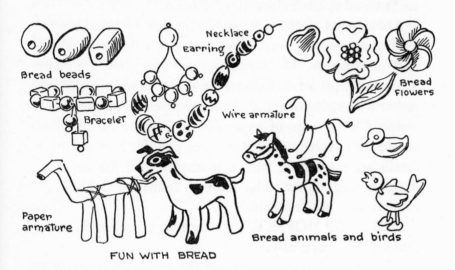

FUN WITH BREAD

to make colorful lapel pins, and can be glued to strips of felt for hairbands, necklaces and bracelets. Flowers can also be given wire stems and leaves, so they can be worn as a corsage or put in a vase.

When starting to make beads or flowers, take a small bit of bread and work it with your fingers for a few minutes. Moisten your fingers if it seems necessary. When the bread is pliable enough, press it into shape. Coloring the bread is done while you are kneading it. Use food colorings and add just a dab of coloring while kneading is in progress.

Make beads by shaping the bread into balls and ovals and running a small nail through the center of each bead. Remove the nail at once and put the beads aside to harden overnight.

Make flowers by modeling the bread into petals and grouping the petals together as needed for the particular flower. Make leaves from small balls of bread. Glue small beads or sequins in the flower centers. When dry, apply a coat of clear varnish or nail polish.

Many animals and birds can be made by modeling balls of bread of different sizes to the shapes needed for the head, body and legs of the animal being made. The head and legs are fastened to the body with toothpicks.

Animals and birds are also made by shaping bread around a rolled newspaper, pipe cleaner, crepe paper or wire "skeleton" or armature. The drawings show how these are made. Skeletons made of newspaper or crepe paper are tied together with string or wire. A wire or pipe cleaner skeleton is wrapped with strips of paper dipped in paste to fill it out before it is covered with bread. Eyes, ears, feathers and other details are marked in with a toothpick, nail file or other sharp-pointed object. The finished animals and birds are colored with poster paints.

DISH MOP MOPPET. Transforming a kitchen dish mop into a doll is quite easy.

Wrap paper around the head of the mop, leaving about an inch of the mop for hair. Tape the paper to the mop handle to secure it. Paint a face on the paper. Dress the moppet in three dish cloths, as shown—one rolled to make the arms, one for a

DISH MOP MOPPET

skirt and one for a blouse. Tie the last two around the moppet's waist with a ribbon sash. You can also dress the doll in a cloth or paper dress, made of a piece 6 inches wide and twice the length of the mop handle. Cut a hole in the center and slip it over the handle up to the head. Tie a ribbon at the waist and one at the neck. Glue paper hands to the arms.

CORNSTARCH DOLLS

CORNSTARCH DOLLS. These dolls have cornstarch heads, which are easy to make and which can also be used for other kinds of small dolls and figures. The body is made of two pipe cleaners, which are twisted together as shown.

To make enough of the cornstarch mixture for two small dolls' heads, mix 1 tablespoon of cornstarch, 2 tablespoons of salt, and 1 tablespoon of boiling water. Heat over the fire for a minute, and then let it cool until you can handle it. Take enough for the head, roll it into a ball, shape it and press it over the pipe cleaner head. Mark in the features with a blunt pencil.

Put the doll aside to dry for at least two days. Then color the features with crayons. Dress the doll in any way you wish.

TOOTHPICK QUICKIES. A quickie is made by pasting a picture to one end of a toothpick. To make them stand up, make a base of four pieces of cardboard glued together. Make holes with a large pin or a thumbtack where you want the

TOOTHPICK QUICKIES

quickies to be, and put the lower ends of the toothpicks in the holes.

One of the nicest things to make is a flower garden of colorful quickie flowers with green paper leaves added, and some quickie butterflies and birds among the flowers. You can make such a garden in a saucer partially filled with soil, and can stick the quickies into the soil. Human faces, comic strip characters, puppies, kittens and any other small colored pictures can be used for other quickies.

PAPER DOILY FANS

PAPER DOILY FANS. These are made from paper doilies and toothpicks. Use a 6-inch doily. Fold it in half, and cut out the center with scissors. Weave a toothpick straight up from A through both thicknesses of paper. Weave two more toothpicks on each side—four in all, and five with the center toothpick. Pull center toothpick down so it is lower than the others. Tape all five toothpicks together and tie with a ribbon bow.

WOODEN SPOON LAPEL PINS. Cut off the handles of wooden ice cream spoons about ½ inch from the bowl. Paint a face on the bowl and add yarn hair or a hat and any other clothing details you wish, such as a cloth neck scarf. Make as many different faces and partial costumes as you can think up or copy from magazine and other pictures. Sew a safety pin to a small circle of felt and glue the felt to the back of the bowl.

WOODEN SPOON LAPEL PINS

WOODEN SPOON DOLLS

WOODEN SPOON TURTLE

Rubber band

WOODEN SPOON PUPPETS

WOODEN SPOON DOLLS. Paint a face on the bowl of a wooden spoon and add yarn hair. Make a cone from a semicircle of white or colored paper, or use a cone-shaped paper cup, and fasten it around the spoon handle. Add a cloth scarf and pipe cleaner or wire arms. Have one hand hold some small artificial flowers.

WOODEN SPOON TURTLE. Cut out a cardboard oval about 4 inches long for the turtle's body and shell. Paint the oval brown and paint black lines for the markings on the shell. Then glue on 5 wooden spoon handles for the head and four legs. Paint them brown and glue on two beads or sequins for eyes.

WOODEN SPOON PUPPETS. It is easy to turn wooden spoons into puppets. Make faces on the bowl with ink, crayons or paints, or paste on colored faces cut from magazines or greeting cards. For a costume, make a hole in the center of a paper napkin. Push the puppet through the hole. Then make two other holes for your thumb and fore-finger.

Make finger puppets from the smaller, flat wooden spoons. Add a face and crayoned or painted clothing, and then fasten the puppet to your forefinger with a rubber band. Make two or three puppets to go on your first three fingers. You can make a puppet theater by cutting a hole in the bottom of a small cardboard box, and then put on a show by having the puppets talk and tell jokes.

PLASTIC CAP FLOWER POTS

PLASTIC CAP FLOWER POTS. These make lovely gifts. Use a large plastic cap. Wedge into the cap a small piece of styrofoam, and stick the stems of small artificial flowers into the styrofoam. Decorate the cap with a ribbon bow.

BUBBLE BATH. All children love bubble baths. Here is how they can make their own. Put a capful or two of a mild liquid detergent in a saucer, and add a little perfume if the detergent is not already scented. Stir the detergent and the perfume with a spoon and then pour the mixture into a bathtub full of water.

KITCHEN CHIMES. Tie a knife, fork and spoon to a ruler or stick. Tap them with a tablespoon and they will sound like melodious musical chimes.

RICE AND MACARONI NAME PINS AND PLACE
CARDS. For the pin base you can use heavy cardboard, felt
glued to cardboard, plastic pin shapes or five or six colored
toothpicks glued together, side by side. Whichever you use,
make the pin measure about 2 inches long and about 1 inch
wide. Pins may be rectangles or ovals.

For a rice name, draw the name in pencil on the pin, and
then cement rice kernels to it, one at a time. Use tweezers if
necessary. With macaroni, use alphabet macaroni letters,
and simply cement them in place. Small safety pins can be
cemented to backs of pins, or you can sew the pins to felt
cut in the shape of the pin and cemented to it. Give the pin
a coat of shellac when it is completed.

Use the letters of alphabet macaroni also to spell out names
on party place cards.

MACARONI FLOWERS. Use shell macaroni and cellophane of all colors. Cut a 2-inch square of cellophane. Lay
the open side of a piece of shell macaroni on a cellophane
square and fold the cellophane over it. Bind the cellophane
tightly with spool wire. This makes one petal. Make three

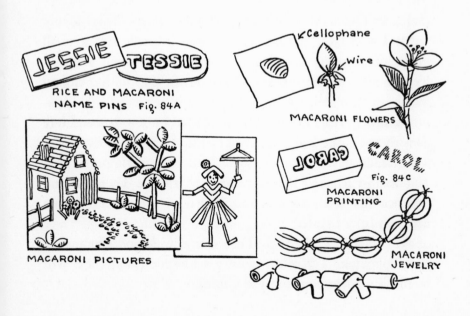

RICE AND MACARONI
NAME PINS Fig. 84A

Cellophane
Wire
MACARONI FLOWERS

MACARONI
PRINTING
Fig. 84c

MACARONI PICTURES

MACARONI
JEWELRY

petals for each flower. Put artificial flower stamens (ten-cent store or hobby store) in the center and bind three petals together with spool wire. Wire a pipe cleaner stem to the wires of the stamens. Wrap green crepe paper or tape around base of the flower. Add two or three artificial leaves. Make eight or ten flowers and bind them together with wire to make a colorful corsage.

MACARONI PRINTING. Print your own name, the names of others or a greeting on letter paper, paper napkins or greeting cards. Use alphabet macaroni and pick out the letters you need. Get a small block of wood and rule pencil lines on it where the bottoms of the letters are to be. Put glue on the wood and press the letters on, arranging them in *reverse order*, so they will read correctly when printed. Sandpaper letters to smooth them. Brush tempera paints on the letters and press the block onto the paper.

MACARONI PICTURES. Macaroni pictures are made by gluing different kinds of macaroni to colored art paper or construction paper. The drawings show how the different kinds can be combined. With a little ingenuity and imagination, you can devise a great many kinds of different pictures.

MACARONI JEWELRY. Elbow macaroni makes interesting three-strand bracelets and necklaces. To make a bracelet, cut three lengths of elastic thread, each twice as long as the finished bracelet. You can also use heavy linen thread or buttonhole twist. Tie the threads together at one end, and coat the opposite ends with fingernail polish to stiffen them for threading.

Thread a piece of macaroni on each thread. Tie a knot to hold the macaroni in place. Keep threading on more macaroni until the bracelet is the right length. Then tie the ends of the threads together. Paint the macaroni with water colors or tempera paints. Necklaces are made in the same way.

The straight macaroni with a hole through the center can

be cut into short sections to serve as beads for necklaces and bracelets. Paint the beads in different colors.

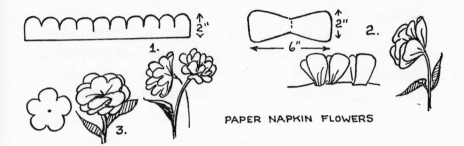

PAPER NAPKIN FLOWERS

PAPER NAPKIN FLOWERS. To make a simple flower, cut a strip about 2 inches wide from one end of a napkin to the other. Scallop one edge of the strip with scissors, and roll or gather the paper to form a flower. For a fluffier flower, lay a second and narrower strip on top of the first one. Twist the middle of an 8 inch length of spool wire around bottoms of flowers to hold them together and to make a double-strand wire stem. The flowers can be colored any color you wish with vegetable dye coloring.

A very pretty rose type of flower is made by cutting four thicknesses of paper napkin into double petals of the kind shown. (Many paper napkins are already folded four thicknesses.) Separate the petals. Double one petal across the middle. Hold it in your left hand and slide one-half of it to the right of the other half, to make two overlapping petals. Pinch the bottoms together. Do the same with the next double petal, putting it to the right of the first two. Add the other two double petals in the same way, and fasten the bottoms of all of them together with the middle of a length of spool wire. Leave the two strands of the wire to form the stem.

So-called spring flowers are made from two or more flower-shaped pieces of paper napkin. Make a small hole in the center of each piece. Slip them onto a 4-inch length of green-covered spool wire, fastening with a drop of glue or cement. Pinch the base of the flower. Then cut leaves and glue them to the stem. Glue beads or sequins in the flower center.

PAPER BAG MASKS. Find a paper bag large enough to fit over your head. Put the bag over your head and cut off enough of the top of the bag to make it rest on your shoulders. Then draw eyes and a mouth and cut them out with

scissors. Make the nose with crayons or paints, or cut a nose-hole. Strands of yarn make good hair.

You can make smiling masks with upturned mouths, and glum-looking masks with downturned mouths. You can also crayon or paint lines on the cheeks and foreheads to create many different kinds of expressions.

PAPER BAG PUPPETS. Use a small paper bag. Draw a face on it or paste on a colored face cut from a magazine. Tie a string around the "neck," leaving enough room for your middle finger. Cut two holes in front of the bag for the arms—your first and third fingers. Add yarn or crepe paper fringe hair, and dress the puppet by pasting on crepe paper or gummed stickers, or by making a crepe paper or cloth dress—a strip of material twice as long as the puppet is tall, with a hole cut in the middle to fit around the neck, and two holes for the arms to pass through.

Another kind of puppet is made like the cat and dog puppets shown in the drawings. Draw the features or paste paper features to the bottom of the bag. Cut a long strip for the mouth. Paste it to the bottom edge of the bag and all the way under the fold so that the mouth will show about ½ inch below the bottom when the bag is folded flat. To make the puppet "talk," slip your hand into the bag, curl your fingers over the fold, and gently open and close your hand. You do not have to make cats and dogs only. You can make any characters you like.

BUNNY BAG. Make these bunny bags at Easter, fill them with Easter grass and candy eggs, and give them to your family and friends. Use a small paper bag. Fold top down to bottom and mark the center point with a pencil. Cut curving lines for ears, as shown. Paint or crayon features. Make whiskers of broomstraws. Glue on a cotton ball in back for a tail. Fill the bag, then close it by pinching each ear together at the bottom and tying with ribbon, yarn or colored cord.

SALT AND FLOUR CLAY. You can make an excellent modeling clay from ingredients found in any kitchen. Mix together 1 cup of salt, ½ cup of flour and 1 cup of water. Heat over a very low flame, and stir constantly until the mixture is thick and rubbery. After the mixture cools, it becomes less sticky and can be molded and modeled just like regular clay. If it seems a little too sticky, roll it in a little flour. You can color this "clay" easily by adding food coloring.

PAPER BAG KNIGHT'S HELMET. To make a very good knight's helmet, all you need to do is cut a paper bag as shown in the drawing, and fold up the part that forms the visor. A decoration can be glued to the front, made of colored paper or tin foil.

PAPER BAG
KNIGHT'S HELMETS

SUGAR SPARKLE GREETINGS. Use granulated sugar, white or colored, to write sparkling letters on greeting cards. Make the cards of colored construction paper that will contrast with the sparkle. Write the greeting one word at a time. Make the letters with colorless nail polish or bottled mucilage, using the brush that comes in the bottle. When you have written one word, sprinkle it with granulated sugar. Finish the greeting one word at a time.

SUGAR SPARKLE
GREETINGS

PAINTING WITH SALT

PAINTING WITH SALT. This is done in the same way as the better known painting with colored sand. With salt, however, you can get finer and more delicate effects. Tint the salt in small bowls with a few drops of vegetable coloring, working the colors in well to make them deeper than needed for the final effect.

Draw or trace a picture on white or colored paper. Coat

all areas that are to be the same color with mucilage, using a brush. Then sprinkle on the salt of the right color, and shake off the excess, saving it for re-use. When the mucilage has dried, add a second color, and so on. Salt pictures are good for framed pictures and greeting cards.

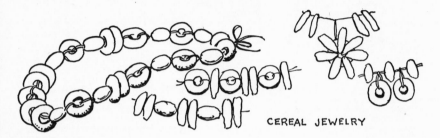

CEREAL JEWELRY

CEREAL JEWELRY. Dry cereal comes in several different forms, as you know. You can string it on heavy thread to make necklaces and bracelets. Use a needle and thread to string the cereals that do not have a hole in the center, and knot the doughnut-shaped ones to the thread if necessary. Paint the cereal beads with tempera paints after they have been strung.